Iconoscope

pitt poetry series

Ed Ochester, EDITOR

iconoscope

new and selected poems

Peter Oresick

EDITED BY Judith Vollmer
INTRODUCTION BY Lawrence Joseph

University of Pittsburgh Press

Published by the University of Pittsburgh Press, Pittsburgh, Pa., 15260

Manufactured in the United States of America
Printed on acid-free paper

10 9 8 7 6 5 4 3 2 1

ISBN 13: 978-0-8229-6380-6
ISBN 10: 0-8229-6380-9

For Stephanie Flom
and for our children
William, Jake, and David

Contents

from *Definitions* (1990)

Introduction / Lawrence Joseph

Peter Oresick's *Iconoscope* is poetry of the highest order. Its breadth and depth of ambition; its sharp-edged, tough-minded intelligence; its intense moral, emotional, and spiritual sensibility; and its acute social consciousness and imaginatively compelling power, all create a body of work virtually singular in American poetry. Oresick's poems are recurrent testimonies to the fact that poetry, in its fullest sense, has to do with vision. Grounded on the entirety of existence and on an experience of the real worlds around and within us, *Iconoscope* strikes deeply into poetry's eternal truths.

The word *iconoscope* (from the Greek εἰκών [*eikōn*], "image," and σκοπεῖν [*skopein*], "to see") entered our language in the 1920s. The iconoscope—invented by Vladimir Zworykin, a Russian-born engineer at the Westinghouse Electric laboratories in Pittsburgh—was the first workable camera in early electronic television. Iconoscope aptly describes Oresick's work. Each poem is a complex object that portrays and allows us to see, in language, images (in the broadest sense) through the determining personality of the poet.

This person—the person, the poet, who speaks to us in *Iconoscope*—was born in 1955 in Ford City, Pennsylvania, a small mill town along the Allegheny River in the western part of the state near Pittsburgh. His grandparents, Ruthenian immigrants, were glassworkers, as were his parents. He grew up in a house three blocks from the factory gate. Baptized in the Catholic Church's Byzantine Rite, he lived one block from each of the town's four Catholic churches: Ruthenian-Ukrainian, Slovak, Polish, and German. Upon graduation from the University of Pittsburgh—where he studied literature as an undergraduate and then received a master of fine arts degree, and where he met his wife, Stephanie Flom—he taught for several years in Pittsburgh public schools, then worked as a full-time father to Stephanie's and his three sons. He then worked in senior positions in literary, scholarly, and technical publishing for over twenty years, while editing two major poetry anthologies that revolved around blue-collar America and the concept of labor in poetry—*Working Classics: Poems on Industrial Life* and *For a Living: The Poetry of Work*. He has also taught literature, writing, and courses on publishing at Emerson College, Carnegie Mellon University, Chatham University, the University of Pittsburgh, and the Pittsburgh High School for the Creative and Performing Arts. After the fall of the Berlin Wall, he lectured on publishing in China, Kazakhstan, and Eastern Europe for the United States Agency for International Development. Furthermore, he is an expert painter in the tradition of Byzantine iconography. Family, ethnic history and identity, industrial work, Catholicism, the geographies of western Pennsylvania and Pittsburgh, immigration and migration, and war-torn histories, including the war on American labor by American capitalism, define and determine *Iconoscope*'s wide-ranging vision.

Definitions, Oresick's first collection, lays the groundwork. There are poems of a father who after four years of combat has nothing to say about it, trembling in his sleep, the poet's mother says, for the next four years. A father who tends a glass furnace, four times on strike, to achieve, by the year the poet was a one-year-old, a few extra cents in his hourly wage. Poems of uncles and aunts, brothers and cousins, close extended families, men and woman of the working class, the valley stretched below them, the river winding its way for miles, the mill fuming, a star igniting above it and burning like a carefully carried candle, before which they cross themselves. In the sixties, the poet, a boy, is given to searching for signs, the sky's crumbling gray clouds, where the blue appeared, like a beautiful eye. He, the poet, in poetry, will say what needs to be said: factories—by the time he is writing poetry and living in Pittsburgh—are mostly closed down, and his father, by this time a pensioner, recites psalms before an icon, addressing praise to the cloudy forehead of God. Images of late August, a maple losing its leaves, iconic for the poet; his wife finding the grave of her father dead ten years; his eldest son set down, crawling in the dimness, pulling himself up on the headstone, touching his fingers delicately to the marble. The poet, in face paint and black tux, balancing a model Cruise missile on a silver tray, a week in prayer and fasting with Molly Rush and Daniel Berrigan, false badges used to enter AVCO Systems Division, banging warhead mounts with tiny hammers, pouring baby bottles of their own blood, singing "Rejoice! Rejoice! Again I say rejoice!"—a voice, often heard inside him, *All shall be well*; a voice his, but not his: *and all shall be well*, *and all manner of things shall be well. No matter what.*

Motifs of Carpatho-Rusyn identity and history, Eastern Rite Catholicism, post–World War II America, Pittsburgh, the working class, icons, poetry, and sociopolitical and sociocultural critical thought are full-blast present in Oresick's spectacular *Warhol-O-Rama*. Andy Warhol, also of Rusyn heritage, of Oresick's parents' generation, of the Byzantine Catholic Metropolitan Church in the United States. Also, of course, of Manhattan, where Warhol singularly changed the worldwide course of visual aesthetics. Oresick identifies with Warhol in ways that no other artist ever has. A serial portrait of the master of serial portraits, *Warhol-O-Rama* is not only an homage to Warhol but also, as a project, a series of poems that mimic Warhol's aesthetic of appropriation and parody. The poems are written—as Warhol paintings are painted—as icons, bringing us into points of resemblance and of difference between the two artists, raising—as both Warhol's and Oresick's work insistently raise—crucial issues of art and culture. Oresick's Warhol is laid to rest from an onion-domed church in Pittsburgh by a Byzantine priest who discovered Warhol as a practicing Catholic at his life's end. Warhol is Oresick's severely tweaked guardian angel, one who collapsed the idea of the grand narrative, a major player in minor things, who, like Oresick, is ever thirsty for images. Oresick's Warhol is the Warhol who said, "Fashions fade, but style is eternal" and "Isn't life but a series of images that repeat?"

Oresick's new poems, all grouped in the first section of the book, "Under the Carpathians," are set on *Definitions*'s and *Warhol-O-Rama*'s common ground. Oresick's Rusyn identity explicitly takes on the quality of both a personal and a global metaphor for a divided homeland, minced and split over centuries, and its language that's disappeared—a "people from nowhere," as Warhol defined them. The poet reports what he sees, the elements of the transnational realities of our time, in images that twist through states of trance. The poet's own household and studio, street and city dissolve at their edges: the body of the ancestral towns interchangeable with that of the twenty-first-century city at the three rivers. The poems move like sliding panels, incandescent with stark character portraits, a surreal inspector, a nun, a beer-quaffing dot.com bureaucrat, and in lyric poem hymns, love poems, and musings on the blurred veils between dreaming and waking. The poet, the iconographer—the last of the Rusyn proletarians, in an America where the state religion is exuberance unregulated and its songbird the iPod, its national pastime a ritualized violence, all things in constant motion, time itself unraveling—remains balanced and sober in his compositions, knowing that when it's over, it's still not over. The poems project a consciousness sensitive to everything—hyperreal, dark and light, ironic and prayerful, ever infused with love. Images—the hilly landscape and the brick houses and the streetlamps lighted on a smoky day, the brittle meadow and the woods mottled with snow, the brook glazed with black ice, the long flat factories, the silent river, crimson clouds, a low-angled sun, redness deepening—painted in words, the poet's feathery brush set down, followed by pressure, drag, lifting quickly: a thin, thorn-like finish, and then his signature. The poem as icon, the icon poem—the poet's iconoscope—a composite mix of different codes and discourses, mediating sensory and cognitive channels, and the objective is the incarnation of the created word.

Lawrence Joseph
New York City
May 1, 2015

Under the Carpathians

I

Reverse Painting on Glass (Kandinsky)

Small-ribbed beings, the lake of bird souls, a lightning strike.
Lowly boats & rowers on blue the color of heaven. A horseman,
masked & sainted, George cubiformed? I think best on the 2nd floor,
window over shoulder, high-back leather chair so rich with feeling.

I report what I see: Kandinsky marshaling 1,000 voices. Flushed
from a winter walk, I hug the desk and dictate the asymmetrical
dream. When yellow vibrates I see the trumpet shape stretch
the full width of the painting, ochre spouting above Kremlin domes,

white horse flying into a sun disk or drumhead, zigzag into a darker
shaman blue. Colors pile. Weblike lines link the main elements.
Turbulence rocks a horse deprived of rider. A lance, an empty halo,
St. George askew—tipped by the evil eye glaring from the lower

quadrant, white abyss the color of silence before birth. I report
resonances, the yapping mouth of Kandinsky. I sit sober. Images twist
through states of trance. My back is stiff, upright, my mind attentive
and waiting for you—your mind stuck on business—for you to finger this

luxurious glass, drops of blue that drip
from the sun. Kiss my forehead. Verify
this report. Lead me downstairs to the pie
warm from the oven & berry blue.

The Inspector

The inspector: middle-aged with flat lace-ups, fatigued
leather case. Her hair dyed auburn & bob cut. She surveys

the property line. My neighbor, a widow, refuses tea.
She's anxious. Tree limbs overhang. Clouds fail to lift

between us. "Stop!" the widow begs me, "Wrong
everything you say." In the street a teal Fiat thrumming.

The inspector looks up, drawn to teal. She looks down,
jots another note. The car dissolves into the curve.

The inspector shakes my hand, shakes the widow's hand.
"Go!" the widow says, "Go!" With attaché & fruit

from the tree in question, the inspector drives off.
I watch her car—not teal—vanish. A horselaugh

erupts from the widow. "She see you no good. Hah!"
Weeks later, from the home office, a letter: "No evidence,

sealed forever." Earsplitting is a widow's fury. Thundery.
Like a wrestler's bicep her naked calves bulge.

She stiffens. I open both my eyes, stare into Cleopatra
eyes. Wind lifts her wig. I hear a faint mechanical whirr.

The rustle of paper. Stop. More rustling of paper.

Lviv, or Lwów

Lwów (now Lviv,
in Ukraine), the glorious
capital city of the Lemko Rusyns
in Galicia, home to the glorious
St. George Cathedral, a city
occupied for centuries by the Polish
overlords of Galicia and all the Carpathians
and their merchant class, the Jews—and when Nikolai
fought with his brother Ivan in 1879
about inheritance of the Oresick land, in our village Królik,
county Sanok;
and when Nikolai won, Ivan Oresick
left and landed a railroad job in Lviv,
now a Rusyn proletarian in the big city of the 1880s
where he lived in the Rusyn ghetto,
and nothing good came out of it,
said his daughter, Mikhailina, who immigrated to the States
after being a DP in Germany for five years after the war,
who visited Pittsburgh each summer
and gave us children candy,
always warning never to trust the Polish,
especially from Lviv, or Lwów (as the Polish mangled it).

Ruthenia

I forget Ruthenia daily, fondly,
daisy chain of mountain hamlets
my ancestors fled—by foot, by rail,
by sail—forswearing Ruthenia: a cloud
of memories drifting from the simmering
peasant pot, or the Cold War

map I hunched above in grammar school.
For 500 years we barely evolved
in stateless Ruthenia, where religion
was the cabbage & the songbird
was the gypsy & the heraldic achievement
was the red bear on hind legs,

its tongue flicking, a field of silver
on the sinister side, stripes on the dexter,
split by the golden trident of Vladimir
the Great, which sounds baronial
but is true, as *The Primary Chronicle* records,
he chose Byzantium over Mecca—

after deliberation with boyars—because
Drinking is the joy of the Rus!
When I return to thee, Ruthenia, I will fly
by way of London, with vodka miniatures
& in-flight movies. I will kiss the earth,
I will peck each cheek—you never unlearn

Ruthenia (& its obsolete ethnonyms)
when your blood is from Ruthenia.
Like playing drinking games. I will forget
America slowly during my sojourn
among the oaks, the lindens, the Carpathian
ash, as I loaf in the undergrowth

& in the mezereum, in the honeysuckle
where I spy voles & black storks & the hazel
grouse, as I sigh aloud. But my mother is
America. I love to live in America where
the state religion is exuberance unregulated
& the songbird is the iPod

& the national pastime is ritualized violence.
It is 5,000 miles & seven centuries from *Rusynsko*
to New York & her beacon hand ablaze.
The land is light & harbor dark & the door
is always open, Ruthenia.
You alone are real to us.

The Meeting

Monday. The boss can barely focus
on the meeting agenda. He sees a new hire
running down the hall. "Chase him down

and give him an agenda." Secretaries rush in,
copy the document, sit the new guy down
at the boardroom table. "This is sweet!

I love agendas, and I always will!
Bring the minutes from the last board meeting."
He keeps on with these demands, for tables & charts,

monthly financials. Now the meeting steams ahead.
It is never like this at the devil's meeting.
No one who has lust, or tasted it,

ever enjoys a meeting. There is a tube
to be attached from the mouth to the ass,
and nothing, still, will ever change in a boss.

He doesn't get it. He's all bulb and no electricity.
All BMW and no gas. The boss now takes orders.
"New hire, do what you think best."

This is how your angel behaves,
this is how your uncle patted you on the back
and said, gee kid, thanks a lot for the help.

A Message about Numbers

At a lodge or warehouse along a creek
near a railroad

in summer. I exited and started walking
when an extravagant town car of some kind
pulled up to me. The driver emerged,
popped the seat forward and motioned

I was wanted by the person in the back
seat. I leaned in and saw Aunt Olga
glowing, healthy, middle-aged,
and smiling, "Hello,"

clearly pleased with herself
and her dramatic entrance
and that she'd surprised me. She said
she came to deliver a message. I felt

the lick of adrenalin and joy, right up
to the base of my skull, knowing
this was an apparition; I was afraid
I was going to wake. She's dead

thirteen months, I calculated, and surely
she must have news about my mother.
Olga said her message was about
numbers, yes, a recession and a puff

of sadness looming ahead, a squeezing,
she said, but "I want you to know

all will be well. OK?"
I laughed. "You came to tell me that?

I don't care about OK, really.
What I really want is how my mother is.
Don't you have a message for me from her?"
She waved her hand. "Your mother's fine,

she's really busy. They have her doing
all sorts of things—I don't even know what.
Don't worry about her."
Not relief, I felt, but puzzlement.

"You didn't have to materialize like Gabriel
to tell me this."
I spit. "You'll be fine," she said.
The driver pulled me away

from the car, flipped the seat
back, pivoted the car around,
driving off along the railroad tracks,
a diminishing cloud of summer dust

at a lodge or warehouse along a creek
near a railroad.

Morning, Allegheny River

Silence. No moon in the heavens.
Stars that spin & pivot, nuanced,

never resting. Again a longing—
forget it. Suddenly, everything is dimly

visible, not yet flushed by dawn.
The bushes dewy, the cinders slick,

the train rails glow light & cold
& bluish. I piss & spit. A breeze

flutters; my body responds with a
shudder of delight. The dog smiles.

I walk along the bank toward home.
Hills greening again, the brown river

sliding under the vapors, the sun up & over
& refracting the black bridge.

No endings. The pure
notes of a car horn ascending.

The Interview

That job? Jesus wept.
Robbed me of my shiftlessness,
that job. Salary + incentives.
I caved. Never battled it

off.

To sit & to phone, to fly,
to conference with booze & nametags.
After steady money, who can forget?
Vicious I was. On time &

stable.

But a hallway holds an echo.
Elevators forget. Soon
I was the memorandum
slid into shredder, so much

confetti.

I didn't realize then.
I had been full. Fullness
preserved me. The earth is firm.
But the sky is a business

analyst.

Curse the sky. Curse the jet.
So the flight ends?

To jet is surrender
anyway. It's a falling

asleep.

Now I'm awake.
Light on my feet.
Ready. To begin.
I feel the emptiness inside.

Buoyancy.

How Dickens Happens

His eruptive dowager chatters to herself,
constructs a confidante of herself,
sarcastic on citizenry who snub or bore
or ignore her. If she resides inside her head
or indulges in snuff,
no one's honor suffers;

if she enjoys a bit of indolence,
no living soul is an atom the worse.
London is hearth, haunt. Hers alone. London
is as complete a solitude as the plains of Syria.
That's neither here nor there, just now.
Dickens marches her home to breakfast,
where having scarcely caught the full flavor
of her first sip of tea, a footman announces
a caller. A gentleman. He stands framed
in the parlor door.
                                        Witness an Englishman
                                        in utter consternation
                                        at the mere presence of her tea things.

Pastoral

There is a path sheep follow among the Carpathians
that does not change. And so it changes. Our people
idling on the meadow crest in cloudless glory

awe-struck, aglow, as if greeting a new bell's arrival
for the church below. Who will explain to them change?
There is a path sheep follow among the Carpathians

under German boot, where our *vatah* built the fire
and he did so without matches, in the Rusyn way
idling on the meadow crest in cloudless glory.

Under Soviets he shaved with a piece of a broken scythe,
leaving his bearded face hollow.
There is a path sheep follow among the Carpathians

where a random wind blows and troubles crumple.
Time itself unravels. Our people root and wallow
idling on the meadow crest in cloudless glory

willow flowers slowly about the pale sparrow.
Exit God and all his orthodox and Moscow's men.
There is a path sheep follow among the Carpathians

idling on the meadow crest in cloudless glory.

When Icons Weep

When icons weep, you are already dizzy
from sin & an urge to run, the gift of tears
seeping up through the hard varnish,

pooling, streaking in rivulets the Virgin's cheek.
(You feel the crimson in your face.) Tears that lack
water or basic salts. Oil-like & redolent. Like myrrh.

Like the chrism given off by the incorruptible
corpses of certain saints. Balanced & sober
is the composition of this icon, despite the massive

left hand. Her face displays a grief contained. Bending
forward, your face a shamanic terror. You're drifting
again . . . toward your own death? Change subject.

What year? Which parish? Why do icons weep?
They're hung under onion domes, the priest grins.
Eta pravada, it's true, from the hour they are blessed

the blest mourn. Hers are the genuine tears of lament.
This church reeks of sweat & lilies & the chicory blue
cloak of the central angel simply radiates

vividness & purity, & when joined with wings
the color of ripe corn, you weep too. This may be your last
time before such a spectacle, & you had dreaded it

because you knew
that when it's over,
it's still not over.

II

That Summer

That summer I loathed beer,
its bitter rinse over the salted tongue.
That August I accepted pinot noir
as a personal savior. I craved its blush
& the notion of the sweet that summer.
I let my son do the grilling,
I didn't need control for once.
That Fourth of July, I ate steak
braised & rare. A sense of fullness.
I passed on desserts the size of planets,
I yapped, I was stupidly satisfied
that summer. Spirited, buff-bodied.
My mind for hours like a Learjet, thrusters
forward to cruising altitude.
I didn't listen. I didn't notice
your death like a train in the distance.
I focused on your breath, your eyes
shifting from ceiling to wall, then closing,
then blinking awake.
I focused on the radio
& its loop of continuous song.
I focused on your eyes—closed again—
your raspy breath, your purple tongue.

Angelism

At Mass my aunt stared at the hymn board,
searching for number patterns, some lucky pair.
She took after her mother, their kitchen love
the Belgian hare roasted, a beet dish. Never a
prayer on Sundays, just Uncle after supper sunken
& snoring in his deck chair. My auntie, my au pair,
sat with me on the sofa—not to watch boxers
square off nor Dr. Kildaire nor a cartoon about
a panda bear but movies about angels like
The Bishop's Wife with Cary Grant, Lucille Ball
in *Forever Darling*, and Jimmy Stewart with slicked
back hair and his angel Clarence, bulbous-nosed,
droll. "Put some pants on, Mike, the bookie
is knocking at the door."

Therapy

When an executive starts therapy
the Board worships him. He stands up
among men, commits to mission
& objectives & strategy. A goal
the Board won't follow, knowing

themselves the trials of the psyche
& how therapy drains, but a goal
nonetheless. No one in this company
is a child. Marx said, "Life is work,
a man's work, and you are men."

Marx is a liar. Children, be children.
You need self, want, & primal motivations.
You will know this when you die.
The knowledge of children is subjective,
ethereal. The fine arts are like an SUV

loaded with helium balloons.
Drive it for pleasure, off road,
toward the goal like class-two
white-water rapids others can't navigate.
That's the business secret of Attila

the Hun, CEO. Never deny
your focus. Money will fall
into your lap. You will lose
your breath. When an executive enters
therapy, The Board worships.

My Father with Pulp Fiction, 1935

Jobless, he enlists with the CCC. At the Allegheny Plateau, bunks
below the canopy of virgin beech, black cherry, hemlock, white pine,

hunkered down in the understory of seedlings & saplings that persists
decades in shade. Eternal juveniles. He sips on the gin; he drums

lightly on the flask draped by his mother's scarf, a Carpathian keepsake.
I watch as his lips move while he reads *Argosy*, how he scans the ads to learn

that one drop of perfume, French label, on the hollow of her neck, loosens
the string of pearls upon a bosom like June rain. If you were fired tomorrow,

if the boss bore down with a grouch, can you get a new job fast? Stop gambling
with the future. Learn electricity. If you were dying tonight and I tendered you

ten more years, you'd grab at it. All I ask is ninety days to shape you. Men are stalled
ability, all too often disguised by ill-fitting clothes. Look the deserving man

you are. Make mistakes in English? Astonishing how many use *who* for *whom*.
Our method provides for correct habits. Send for our book *Muscular Development*.

Look better. Last longer. *Crack! His fist lands squarely behind the ear and down
the chump drops in a quick heap. He pivots to face another—thud.*

Another limp form lies on the ground. Father, quivering, tense,
stands over the prostrate goons, waiting for them to shift or twitch.

But they don't. The drink, they say, of expatriated Ukraine is crude alcohol
& water, & its intemperance is a tranquil madness

purely criminal in a less childlike people.

My Father Who Art in Heaven

I bamboozled you just a little
says the dream of my dead father.

The curtain rose for years
on the Plate Glass Works

on one who, counting out days
of boredom & ribbons of glass

& the passing weather, daily
declared his intention of drowning

all troubles in prayer. Churchgoers
enter single file, in dress suits & fedoras

to the toll of a pealing bell. Poker games played
for nickels draw down the coughing ushers

to the basement. Why do we look
with anger & chagrin? We admire Jesus H.

Christ, but we don't behave, do we?
The hilly landscape & brick houses

& streetlamps lighted all the smoky day.
I was not anaesthetized, Father, to its attractions.

The most obvious sex appeal of any town
I have known. Its structural & ornamental iron

works, its Crucible Steel Company of America,
its roller bearing, its pipe bending, its smelting

till we all fall unconscious. My dead father in heaven
grows sadder & sadder as he drinks. Soon he will read

the tender passages from a Western by Zane Grey,
the one from his World War II Red Cross package—

soap, razors, a deck of cards. He stood night watch
& thought of her. Don't forget to pay the mortgage,

he wrote. Here & now my wheelchaired mother
in senior care. Me pushing. The television at the end

of the hall like a headlight—a star accelerating
the dementia. A full moon rises up,

at first like a disk of cheap china, washed-out tints.
The pale yellow vanishes and drains it paler still.

The brittle meadow & the woods mottled
with snow. The skeletons of trees. The brook glazed

with black ice. The long flat factories. The silent river.

Franklin

Who doesn't live a life fouled by Franklin?
God helps them that help themselves.
When the well's dry, well, we know the worth

of water. Beer is proof that God loves us.
Years ago, before we were born, when fish
& visitors stunk in three days, she that fell in love

with herself had no rivals. Time was money.
Three kept a secret if two of them were dead.
Publisher, printer, polymath. Nothing said

to be certain except death & taxes. O myth
of a nation. Little strokes fell great oaks.
Tales told to children slumped & dreamy.

There is no little enemy. Never was a good war
or a bad peace. Scientist and inventor. Bifocals,
Franklin stove, the lightning rod to catch the light

overflowing with Franklin. Why is the text fouled
with Franklin? Diplomat. Minister to France.
Time was something that fed on fire. Candlemaker

too. Postmaster general, founded the first fire
department, first public library, the fire couldn't catch
its breath or hang on for life. Political writer, activist,

linguist fluent in five languages, abolitionist, eating not
to dullness & drinking not to elevation.

I Can't Hear

I can't hear when I'm sleeping.
I fear the stalker, the tomb
robber, the contractor who
measures my sleeping soul.

His hatred,
my tomb.

Let this wall be my tongue.
I am always awake, sick of your chatter
& your noxious grin.

You ignore the evidence,
you don't know the procedures.
You make it up as you go.

I can't hear you. My ears are deaf
to your monologues. You exist but
I never seek you out. I can fend for
myself. My portfolio is slowly
growing.

I know what to do:
Keep silent. Everyone will walk away
in time, abandoning me like a corpse
at the lip of a grave.

This is science. This is living.
Only a set of genes like my mother's
could foretell a life like mine.

I don't know these punks.
I can't hear their music.
My brain can't hear. Seek
the enemy & flush him out.
Hate is a boom box blaring
from a block away, daring you
to silence the music.

Autumn Evening at the Window with Brushes

Crimson clouds, a low-angled sun, redness deepening.
It's an art to see shapes in clouds or spot a silhouette.
At the end of a painting lesson, I am contented by the gurgle
of faucet & soap. I love working brush bellies with thumb
& forefinger, rinsing, scraping the ferrule with my nails,
swabbing blotter cloth till no more pigment dislodges, or
I repeat the massage. Sable martens boast a belly that wicks,
reservoirs the paint, allows a painter to increase pressure
and broaden a line so the pigment flows slowly, evenly,
composing sleek curves. Clouds drift, unravel. I dress
a clean brush to original form, tip needling to a point. Finest
sable is Kolinsky of northern Siberia, where cruel climate breeds
hair that's robust yet supple. Springy, absorbent. Kolinsky sells
at the price of gold factored thrice, as old Soviets said, the cheap
brushes a false economy. I favor plated-nickel ferrules, corrosion-
resistant. I like bristles to taper & edge. I like best the sign-
liner for gypsy teardrop strokes, my feathery brush down, followed
by pressure, drag, lifting quickly: a thin, thorn-like finish:
my signature. I rotate the brush ninety degrees and repeat
without reloading the Kolinsky. It's a tool I work methodically yet
without method, seemingly, and Mars red unbinds like a spirit
emulsified. Red runs the slop sink in rivulets, ruby hues spotting,
sticking to the stainless steel, hunching, blobs like big-headed
embryos with bantam hands & warm hearts & naive metaphysics
dashed by force of water until they sail alone
without left or right brain or even a single, bridging thought.
Color drains & cycles into endless forms.
Sable brushes stand on handles, not on their heads.
They dry naturally in a jar on a windowsill
giving best results when cared for properly
& last a lifetime.

She Whispers

She whispers into my room
which I've abandoned.
There was my chastity and my virtue
until I couldn't live without you.
You don't want me.
You ignore me and taunt me.
You remember the way I'll be.
The stream trickles and dries up
in the cold at winter's end,
in the cold of my rambling mind.
All emotion dries up
in my rambling mind.
It is like a mute button on the remote,
like a straight jacket. It is a dim ember
at noon in the valley far below,
this longing for you.

III

To a Museum Guard at Shift Change

From the café, beneath the double flight of marble
stairs, I watch your right foot plant, the left scrape
its sole, see the vapors trailing you: undead, unemployed
from the lofty rooms of bronze statuettes, oils
of nudes & clusters of nudes, watercolors of unkempt

meadows. You, through the mist of the Romanesque
fount, are my Muse descending. I climb past you, smile,
and claim your abandoned station. I was here first,
years ago. A gray spring day. My mother chaperoned.
We queued along a velvet rope, ticketed, in a line

twisting for *Whistler's Mother.* Solemnity. Reward.
Then tiptoed the balustrade to these cascading stairs.
What I remember now is my mother's plumpness.
The buttons of her Sunday coat, her delicate aroma.
I gripped her wrist, still a boy, not yet restless

or private or spooked by dreams of loss, still a boy
and consolable, my hand in her hand fused.
Our feet, in tandem, descended the imperial
stairs, & the fountain spewed & splashed.
The hushed angel in a tapestry bore witness

to how she shushed me past the drowsy guard—alight
on the edge of his folding chair, precarious
on the landing—then swiftly toward the loose-breasted
twin goddesses, on twin pedestals, who lift
globes of light beside the colossal doors.

Origins of the Ruthenian

Know your place. No one has ever found
a linguistic kin of Ruthenian—Hutsul, Boyko, Lemko—
though once someone studied the blood as a key
to the origins of Mr. Danko's teeth & skull, asserting
the head was not built like that of other men—
Lapps, Turks, or German Jews. Our thoughts are ragged.
There is only one bottle of beer that can make us vacate our minds.
All sadness is the same. Mary found herself in her frustration
with Jesus. Don't imbibe in the absence of sinners.
No thing, no person is empty of sadness.
Don't judge. Drink with abandon.
No beer will make you tipsy. Don't be choosy,
abstain from beer that doesn't rock you
like a car sailing when it loses it brakes.

At the Crypt of the Church of Our Lady of the Veil

in Lviv, hear ancestral skulls
murmur. *Beer.* Dusky amber?
Pale pilsner? "Quit thirsting
for the sacred blood," they say.

"Stack our bones or fling them
skyward—worship beer.
Quaffed, sipped, sucked,
articulated, & aspirated beer

of the Most Holy Theotokos."
Skull puzzlement. Like the face
of a snow leopard circling
the ringmaster, the Alpha

Male. "O mesmerized pilgrim,
full of credit: More beer!"
I hoist pitchers, pour into yaps
& guts & the slate-black sea.

I swim toward Anonymity
in beer. Like a lunatic flailing,
springing out of one's skin.
Every head, every tongue

shall ache. For what? Gusto!
Pensioners circle the Soviet
neon on the blink: Cold. Beer.
Skull is a town crier: Hear ye!

All of you shall die. Even lords
of high decision can't defuse
beer sentiment, its looping
mantra that quivers pilgrim knees.

For all desire to do good—
For all the obscene profits—
For all right ways of thinking—
Repent. Don't wait to cross over.

When in 2009 the G20 Summit Convened in Pittsburgh

Look who's whistling through bleached teeth now,
one hand on svelte hip, one fist pumping the air—
Pittsburgh—once that madcap & zany joke factory

now chosen for her fetching comeback tale
& her earth-sheltered welcome center
& her Warhol & her Tropical Forest Conservatory

& her Rosemont, working farm of the moguls
of ketchup. Rarely since the global credit crisis
do Pittsburghers cross bridges or rivers or the thresholds

of stunningly profitable ventures. Yet tonight,
as global output contracts at a pace not seen since
the 1930s, as the French president proposes reform

of the International Monetary Fund & the US
president delights in the local crepes with crispy edges,
& as Greenpeace commandos drape a WHAT THE FUCK?

banner from the deck of the West End Bridge
(above which Chinook & Black Hawk helicopters hover),
& as police use the LRAD sound cannon on protesters
for the first time in the United States or Canada—

a Pittsburgh Pirate homers into the Allegheny River
& sets the esplanade ablaze with the flash
& fizzle of fireworks launched at the flat lozenge

of the moon, a ghostly azure, suspended low
above the sweep of the cantilevered roofs
on the opposite shoreline—the poured concrete,

the glass towers, the obelisks—a costly parody
of bygone days when confidence in the future, evinced
by our sixty miles of integrated mills, was illustrated

by a time capsule, a chamber "hermetically" sealed
in Steel City alloys, bicentennially filled with newsprint
& artifacts of 1958 Pittsburgh to be cracked open

& savored in some distant epoch, an idea first
embraced by Esarhaddon, son of Sennacherib, king
of Assyria, Babylonia, & Egypt, & reenacted now

in waves of sound & light—the roar of fireworks night
for a losing franchise, the hoarse voices of Pittsburghers—
wafting into the void, accelerated by Jupiter's pull,

& then hurled by Jupiter out of the solar system,
yet another urban missive from a noisy planet,
a comingling of mathematics and human music, charming

& powerful, a murmur preserved of our city-state
that once flourished—before its citizens dispersed
to other lands, to greater deeds on the blue Earth.

What the Hermit Zosimus Said

I curse like an Argonaut when I'm alone.
I pray. I rise briefly. I sit and pray again.

After contemplation, I'm sleepy, I'm ready
to curse again. Only slowly do I lose all

desires. I barely change. A rock is a rock
forever. The sea is the sea. I never lose

the self.
                So Diocletian & Galerius returned

to Antioch, where the emperors partook
in the blood ritual of a haruspex,

who, when the entrails confounded him,
stood and prayed to Apollo, then sat and prayed

again, cursing like an Argonaut.
A rock is a rock forever.

Sister Rosaire Kopczenski Enters the Religious Life

I hugged my death like a child.
I was a trunk. Rooted, bearing down,
squeezing.

I pulled my death—an only child—
tightly to my bosom. We were both dark
and deeply rooted.

When the crow cawed, the soldier snarled
and a door swung open, but we
bore down and embraced.

When the horse snorted, the soldier stomped
and a door slid open, but we
stood solidly and clinched.

When diplomacy failed again, the land retreated
and realigned under a new flag. Historians assessed
the mud and the dead and the blood, and I pulled

my death—an only child—even tighter
to my bosom. A trunk, I bore down
and I squeezed.

The Old Anarchy

The new anarchy says the sober will agree
on everything, kiss & make up.
The fighter is equally good. She leaps into the air.
While floating there, suspended, loses
nothing but her time.

This morning the sun left us its beer cans from the night
before. I don't believe in omens, & got on
with my drive to work, descending into the parking
garage. The garage is a tomb. I feel nested.
Everything is orderly. I have work to do.

My heart is serene & rested at my desk,
my monastery. Look at me.

IV

Paper Plates

Forget the thumb dents on the mottled cheese,
or how the bread got foul, & this dull knife.

Forget how the wind whips sand to damn your eyes
and ants march precisely in procession.

Your mother fed you, at times, from paper plates.
Paisley plates won't hold your mother's face,

they assumes aspects, according to memory,
continuous tones of black & white & black.

A picnic is no picnic. See the dune view, the girdling
line of the horizon, how stars fade-in at dusk.

Remember your mother, dived-down in the churchyard
grasses, breaking up, once & for all, the charmed

family circle.

I Hiked the Carpathians

I hiked the Carpathians hexameter by hexameter,
yet couldn't find the source text I was looking for:
"The Four Idylls," the first verse to laud Nature
in Mitteleuropa. I was four hundred years too late to bird-watch

the ancestral life: piety & moiling & submission.
Over the mountains, a pale-green sky.
A thousand years seemed to retreat. I colonized
the taverna, its red corner, & ate my beet soup,

mulling my own primitive outlook, while Ruthenia hid
among the treetops, leaves rustling, as in the saga
where our people don't exist yet. Only thick black trees
in an autumn light, & that first, biting frost.

Fired//On My 49th Birthday

After the firing, after the boxed drawers,
the perp walk to the parking lot,
the acids of shame, the frankness of banks,
after gin & tonic, DVDs, golf without end,
a new normal grows.

After the cheap promises
of billboards, after habit, memos,
quarterly sales, busted copiers,
accountants materializing like Scrooge's Marley,
after trade shows, after my kids get a car
& buy their own clothes,
a new normal grows.

Health care is swilling profits, personal days.
Unemployment insurance is calling in her little ones,
"Come home, Come home!" May sheep balls,
may the ferocity of sheep driven to holiness,
may the repose of their hung bellies come
& a new normal grow.

May the sweet kinks of the fist, may the full flower
of the hamstrings, the thorax,
"Bow Down." Come "Rise Up,"
come new normal:

> my five arms and all my hands,
> all my white sins forgiven,
> my car passing under the stars
> now normal. May my children inherit.

Mary, Mary

My old mother Mary spied the Virgin
Mary—shouted: "I like that face!"

Buddha-bellied, droop-breasted,
wheelchaired octogenarian.

Mother tethered, Mary docked
at her nightstand:

votives & icons, votives & icons.
The stink of dementia. O Lourdes:

Teen shepherds spied a vapor.
So what? Flesh matters.

Vision matters. Bury your dead.
Silence the silver bells, the choir

all in a row, muffle the priest,
muffle the mourners shuffling past

the snuffed candles as they return
to idling autos, muffled too

the morning she crosses over
house to hearse to cemetery sod.

No shouting from the worms,
please. No roses, no roses

in the yawning grave.
Dim the sun.

No bird chirp. No tree
with generous shade.

In the contiguous field, no tractor.
No mournful cows loitering.

No raucous rooster's crow.
No bells pealing. No candles.

No incense curling.
Don't eat the luncheon meats.

Unshout the noise that banished
Mary. Mark the day of her cold

feet—after the stroke, after
the split skull, after the plaqued

brain release. Of my mother Mary,
who spied the Virgin Mary, whose face

I pray she likes.

My Mother's Pirohi

She simply boils, like most everyone, potatoes
till tender, drains well and adds butter, salt, sharp
cheese during the mash. The bread board on hooks,
wrapped in an old bed sheet, is carried up

cellar stairs by yours truly. I stare at the bowl
mostly, and sifted flour blending with yolk and milk,
oil and water, slow to reach consistency. Beyond her,
the kitchen's heat dissolves the latticework

of frost on six window panes. She usually hums
along radio songs while she kneads three minutes,
lightly dusts with flour and kneads again. She opens
door, sets bowl on the back porch to chill.

In large sauce pan, with onion, at medium blue
flame, she melts butter eight minutes, maybe ten,
and blends with potato filling. I bring back dough
and roll to approximately five millimeters (because

at age twelve I believe millimeters are the future
in America). I cut into circles, roughly seven
centimeters in diameter, with glass, drinking glass
with decal of New York. A souvenir, a habit

I can't fully explain. As I carve circles, she kneads
excess, rerolls, and we repeat. A dollop
of filling in the middle, filling in the middle
of each circle and brush with egg white. She hums

through this too, folding over and pinching edges
with the fork. In a pot of boiling salted water, cook
the pirohi two minutes before draining and setting aside.
In saucepan butter-coated she fries them slowly until

golden then serves with sour cream and browned onion.
At table, as far as I can recall, there was never green
salad or vegetable, only pirohi and that woman
about forty, humming, who won my heart by her love for pirohi.

This the Very Coinage of My Brain

How to survive the money dream from childhood, in which
strong boys push me down, or boys younger & more feisty, where
I lose balance & allow knees to buckle & go with the flow of rolling
over & over on the lawn, where a second earlier I was Hank Aaron
or Clemente or goofing with a rival boy tribe. Wrestling a dream
into middle age: good luck or bad? My heart races, I spill again
ass backward onto stacks of quarters & nickels & dimes, rolling
& raking them from the trim, rich grass.

How profound that coins may save
our souls & lend immediate mercy & peace. Coins reformulate
rigid opinions, our restlessness, coins allow us to be submissive
to the faint, struck image of presidents. An effigy of a dead president
is the president, a material thing, and the image of an Indian head
is an Indian. The form of Lincoln is always Lincoln. Lincoln bleeds
a peasanty blood, and our peasants' blood runs a touch blue.
I rake coins, I stuff pockets. Copper & silver never devalue.
If money isn't distributed, I dishonor it. I'm an honorary man
when I'm moneyed; devils flee. I wake, I make macabre
images that frighten no one as I walk with coffee the Stanton Avenue
of ramshackle homes, where mothers never flinch, and porch sit, stolidly.
Now the street widens with respectability. My looping dream longs
to make a coin noise in my pocket & escape limbo. Neighbors listen
with a broad smile & wink: "More coins under the sidewalk, the hill,
the river. Coins are under all over." I talk with folks when I'm stopped,
but I walk alone through the biggest coal district in the country, where
each night I sleep high above ground, morning slipping back into bones,
stacked with flat presidential visages. I gaze into their death
masks, they scrutinize mine, all of us symbols of the visible order,
partaking of grace according to faith in these United States

where we are all having a dream together. At Lincoln's deathbed
the war secretary uttered, "Now he belongs to the ages." Or was it
"To the angels"? I can't remember how the civics teacher said it,
or why I chose it, just that Edwin Stanton was a Pittsburgh lawyer
& Presbyterian & Lincoln's secretary of war,
& once he lived in that house seen clearly from my third-floor window,
if only I could get up, instead of rolling over, for another solid sleep.

I Love To Sleep Curled

I love to sleep curled on the edge
under her arm, unlicensed
& weaving in the spectral,

chromatically climbing
the twelve tones, just a boy
in the air again, face to the stars,

soaring, sailing soberly,
watched by worshiping faces.
I swear by heaven of the dream

arts. I trust the body arched
& soaring, & the pure
labor of the dream,

not the usual grief
of the nation, localized, yowling
from the mouth, just the ripest

of dreams now dropping, now
pouring like rain through hair,
shampooing this sleep

seeping into the honeycomb,
into the well, into the silent
language of the gorgeous—

while I curl on the edge—
her arm above me, the pillow cradled
beneath my chin.

The Ruthenian Lamb

I.

I remember the grand interior of the Kazakhstan Union of Writers, endless toasting with caviar and vodka and horse meat pâté. Chased with beer. Strange place for me to be? Further East, into the endless steppes, post-Soviet. Like the Carpathian space inversed. I remember yogurt and fermented mare's milk and chai. Ground zero of *First Lightning* that launched the arms race. Thirty-six nuclear warheads—stored poorly and vulnerable to smugglers—dehydrated of uranium by U.S. technicians. Then a president's decree: "One more threat of nuclear proliferation removed. Today is a good day for a cultural exchange!" By this time, the publishers and writers of the new republic loved us Americans and the seminar ended.

II.

Black Land Rovers hauled us to the high country, behind a printing plant, to the large yurt where dozens of factory workers waved American flags. A Ruthenian lamb was tethered to a spike. Our host's employees loaded casks with spring water and stropped a blade against a stone, a noise that rushed the dogs into a frenzy, the lamb divining something as well and bleating. The fire pit with a kettle roiling, our host grasped the lamb's rear legs and jerked upward, the lamb digging in front legs on a spot on the grass. He tossed it onto its back, bound the front legs with twine, holding a back leg under his knee so I could clasp down the head by its ears. Dividing the wool to the left of the breastbone, he slit the hide, exposing an inner lining of fat that swelled with organs. No blood rose out.

III.

The lamb lay still, and he formed his right hand fingers together into a point and drove them deep into the abdomen of the lamb, along the inside of the ribs to the spine where he felt the main artery with his forefinger, plucked it once and severed it. He removed his hand slowly, did not spill a drop of blood, the lamb passing into coma. When the eyelids no longer twitched, he flicked his finger against them. Dead. Then the legs were snapped at the knees, set aside for the head soup. He stripped back the hide in four directions and weighed it down with rocks, in order to carve, the belly up and glistening white and fatty. Only a patch of wool remained on the sternum. Not to be touched.

IV.

He leaned carefully over the lamb and clenched the strip of woolly hide with his teeth, rocking, pulling the patch away from the carcass. Only then could he touch it with his hands, and he gave it to a crone, who dropped her bouquet of wildflowers and began the carving. I opened my notebook and asked the name of each part, each organ, and I learned fifty new words. Later, the bubbling cauldron filled with hot blood stew, he hooked the meat. He cut out the eye for me, the guest of honor.

V.

He handed me the knife and I sliced small wedges of fat, a piece for each member of the publishers union, in descending order of age, as protocol demands. "Petro, Petro, sing us a Rusyn song!" There they stand, even now, in the waxing dark. And so I yield and sing to them, who pass the small silver plate. In front of me now, lucent and moist, the eye of the lamb. The yurt top expresses a deep red glow, the steppe winds stir, the factory workers peer inside to watch me, and I eat.

from *Warhol-O-Rama*
(2008)

Andy Warhol for Gods Who Must Be Crazy

Wow! Watch Warhol catch lightning in a bottle
in 1962—a Coca-Cola bottle! Pop on pop!

Lord, have mercy

This slaphappy, totemic pastiche of goofy
pratfalls & art gags metastasized

Lord, have mercy

into an unlikely international smash, staring
the Rusyn American whom the gods elect

Christ, have mercy

to play the lead role, the completely ingratiating
Andy Warhol. He plays an idiot savant

Lord, have mercy

unaware of high culture, who finds a Coke bottle
in lower Manhattan. His life is spun around

Lord, have mercy

by this mystical object. As with most Warhol
movies, it looks slipshod, even amateurish at times,

Christ, have mercy

yet its attitude is so bubbly it's hard to resist, proving
visual comedy remains a true international language

Grant it, O Lord

that millions around the world drink up.

Andy Warhol for Short Attention Spans

Andrew Warhola: working-class Pittsburgh Rusyn immigrants Roaring '20s St. Vitus' Dance sickly albino mama's boy fan boy Schenley High Carnegie Tech pictorial design major "Success is a Job in New York City" *Vogue* shortened his name (WAWR-hawl or WAWR-hohl?) Campbell's Soup cans disasters Elvis icons Marilyn Monroe The Silver Factory 16mm films *Chelsea Girls* is not easy to watch Valerie Solanas assassin clinically dead Exploding Plastic Inevitable *Interview Magazine* then painting again Maos skulls commissioned portraits in Polaroid MTV *AW's 15 Minutes* Rorschachs collaborations with Basquiat Last Suppers following routine gall bladder surgery 1987 his Byzantine Catholic burial Route 88 cemetery memorial mass St. Patrick's New York crass estate wrangling MOMA retrospective 1/2 billion $ valuation Warhol Bridge Warhol Museum now dead art icon with a half-life of plutonium.

Andy Warhol for Catholics

The discovery of Warhol
as a practicing Catholic
at his life's end, combined
with the many works of art
ready-made from Da Vinci's
The Last Supper, has led
some to argue the extent
to which he was a spiritual
artist. The question is knotty.
If we understand spiritual
simply to mean a concern
with things beyond
the merely material, then
spiritual art is a pure
tautology. After all, if painting
isn't in some sense spiritual,
then it isn't Art.
It's just paint.
He was laid to rest
from an onion-domed church
by a Byzantine priest
who discovered Warhol
as a practicing Catholic
at his life's end, combined
with many works of art.

Andy Warhol for the FBI

1. Agent [redacted] and I attended the San Francisco Film Festival midnight screening of the picture *Lonesome Cowboys*, an Andy Warhol Production shot in Arizona.

2. Warhol was absent, but an actor spoke on his behalf in a senseless monologue about not knowing whether to put the beginning of the movie at the end or vice versa.

3. The movie opens with a cowboy practicing a ballet. A conversation ensues regarding the misuse of mascara by another cowboy. It is difficult to understand the words being spoken, partly due to the poor audio and partly to the actors' poor enunciation. We also suspect there was no script.

4. Later the cowboys go out to the ranch, take a woman (Viva) from her horse, remove her clothes, and assault her. Her privates are exposed; she lies on her back and an actor kneels near her shoulders with his face in the vicinity of her genitals, but a second actor blocks the view. According to the program notes, "Viva's languorous seduction is actually a satirical comment on sexual artifice."

5. In another scene Viva dares a cowboy to take off his clothes and join her in nudity, yet their discussion centers on the Catholic Church's liturgical songs. She finally prevails. There are movements and gyrations; however, at no time does the camera show penetration or a position for insertion.

6. Many of the cast portray their parts as if in a stupor from marijuana, drugs, or alcohol. Obscene words, phrases, and gestures occur throughout the film. There is no plot, no development of characters, just a remotely connected series of scenes that depicted sexual relationships of a homosexual and heterosexual nature.

7. We cannot ascertain whether an actual rape occurs onscreen. We submit, therefore, that a full investigation into the transportation of pornography (the exposed negative) across state lines will lead nowhere.

Googlism for Andy Warhol

Andy Warhol is a dialect of Ukrainian
Andy Warhol is lost in my lava lamp
Andy Warhol is lurking at his own party like Gatsby
Andy Warhol is loathe to say how much he's raking in
Andy Warhol is appropriating images
Andy Warhol is the first chapter in an old American story
Andy Warhol is to culture what strip mining is to West Virginia
Andy Warhol is famous for creating the character Andy Warhol
Andy Warhol is slowly beginning to recall his past life
Andy Warhol is short on words

Andy Warhol is Pope of Pop
Andy Warhol is expressing himself with capitalist commodity fetishism
    with wit and camp good humor
Andy Warhol is too nice a man to be president
Andy Warhol is a chip off the old Dada
Andy Warhol is the Bill of Rights for inanimate objects
Andy Warhol is a painter whose works do not call for interpretation
Andy Warhol is pronounced clinically dead
Andy Warhol is one of many American celebrities at Tokyo Wax Museum
Andy Warhol is seduced by the idea he could have a soul of his own
Andy Warhol is Art minus art

Andy Warhol is New York City's smallest borough
Andy Warhol is just one example of how a star is born
Andy Warhol is deviating from slavish copying of inherited Byzantine forms
Andy Warhol is the only genius I've ever known with an IQ of 60
Andy Warhol is based on a true story set mainly in the '60s
Andy Warhol is a spunky teenager who with pal Philip Pearlstein sets out to find
Andy Warhol is offering rebates when you purchase any 5 cans of Campbell's soup

Andy Warhol is not responsible for the actions of third parties
Andy Warhol is one of our private jokes—shorthand to goof on obsessive behavior
Andy Warhol is the lunatic with only one idea

Andy Warhol is the Carpathians' highest peak at 2,061 m
Andy Warhol is where the peasants truly believe in vampires
Andy Warhol is Napoleon in rags in Dylan's "Like a Rolling Stone"
Andy Warhol is a robot yet puts his painterly mark on his mechanical process
Andy Warhol is true to ambiguity
Andy Warhol is almost certainly why I always wanted to be in show business
Andy Warhol is the international gesture for *%&#!
Andy Warhol is suppressing the personal in a marathon essay on boredom
Andy Warhol is a swell costume for theme parties and masquerade
Andy Warhol is asking me to take him home

Andy Warhol is as good as the genre gets
Andy Warhol is prince among the dead celebrity moneymakers
Andy Warhol is available for sale or resale to any and all
Andy Warhol is a blue-collar town of steel mills & rabid football fans
Andy Warhol is just another weird manifestation of the American
  mania to absorb all into the soft, pulpy wad of pop culture
Andy Warhol is having a near-life experience
Andy Warhol is reality's mirror so try drawing something banal
Andy Warhol is a sphinx without a riddle
Andy Warhol is played in blond by the dead funny Tony Curtis
Andy Warhol is a rich subject to talk about

Andy Warhol is struck by lightning up to 50 times each year
Andy Warhol is my guardian angel severely tweaked
Andy Warhol is the cradle of these folk tales

Andy Warhol is a lovely dog but he is just not himself these days
Andy Warhol is bound to give assent to all that the Church teaches
Andy Warhol is beyond amazing, as is his wife Jan
Andy Warhol is a Slavic racial type from Pittsburgh
Andy Warhol is an exception to that rule
Andy Warhol is full of surprises for the uninitiated
Andy Warhol is making you dreamy

Andy Warhol is not often recognized as a key asset to Washington
Andy Warhol is canoodling with Capote in a corner banquette
Andy Warhol is to Norman Rockwell what Judas is to Jesus
Andy Warhol is boy king of mythic Ruthenia
Andy Warhol is the beneficiary of some seriously low expectations
Andy Warhol is owned and ultimately managed by its shareholders
Andy Warhol is a hammer—everything's a nail to him
Andy Warhol is just one of many stars to leave hand and foot in cement
Andy Warhol is more is better
Andy Warhol is a hoot as an Asian

Andy Warhol is the idea of the collapse of grand narratives
Andy Warhol is a water sprite turned human turned water sprite
Andy Warhol is the confluence of the Allegheny and Monongahela
Andy Warhol is tomato-soup-can-boy in *I Shot Andy Warhol*
Andy Warhol is uncapping an ad blitz for loyal ketchup customers to *pour out*
Andy Warhol is vivid in its historical reality but forces yawns
Andy Warhol is an idiot savant well I don't know about the savant part
Andy Warhol is voluptuously amusing as a girl on a husband hunt
Andy Warhol is most often explained by the masochism of diva worship
Andy Warhol is famously famous for being famous

Andy Warhol is the vapor trail of American experience
Andy Warhol is the hub of East Slovakia & Transcarpathian Ukraine
Andy Warhol is viewed as something of a spent force in certain circles
Andy Warhol is a sucker for Sandra Dee in *Tammy Tell Me True*
Andy Warhol is one of the more profitable purveyors of distraction owned by media goliath Viacom
Andy Warhol is dramatized in all his brilliance on this quartz movement wall clock
Andy Warhol is within a day's drive of half of the United States
Andy Warhol is why the terrorist hate us
Andy Warhol is copyrighted and cannot be reproduced without consent
Andy Warhol is a way of thinking that so far has eluded precise definition

Andy Warhol is no soup can
Andy Warhol is never mentioned in scripture
Andy Warhol is not enjoying a post-game beer and masculine camaraderie
Andy Warhol is ignoring what they write just measuring it in inches
Andy Warhol is a major player in minor things
Andy Warhol is one of many artists we can deliver at a discount
Andy Warhol is more American Dream than historical figure
Andy Warhol is an optimist—he believes that citizens, given equal opportunity, earn the right to fame
Andy Warhol is one of those people in my life I would love to give something back to
Andy Warhol is a hospital where the beds must remain empty

Andy Warhol is not going to be at the party

Andy Warhol for the Taj Warhol

What thoughts I have of you tonight, Andy Warhol, for I canoed with heartburn down the shimmery Allegheny watched over by a saffron moon.

In my deltoid fatigue, and thirsty for images, I docked beneath your bridge and walked Sandusky Street to Taj Warhol, dreaming of your seriality!

What auras! My third chakra shuddered! Students in a Warhol posse cruising galleries on a Friday night! The foyer filled with grunge bands! Babies in Archives! Yuppies in Café! Coughing scholars in the dim Theater!— and you, Norman Rockwell, what were you doing in the Silver Cloud room?

I saw you, Andy Warhol, mesmerized, rummaging in the gift shop among the branded tchotchkes: Warhol PEZ Dispensers! Bobbleheads! Warhol dog toys!

You fingered hackey sacks & zipper pulls & cork screws & sports bras & action figures & lunchboxes & boom boom sticks & jar openers & bingo chips & day planners & shot glasses & yoyos. Warhol yoyos!

I heard you ask a sales associate: Who de-beered the Beercan Koozies? What price Warhol Chia? When the camouflage condom?

I wandered the luminescent aisles following you, and followed in turn by the lone guard tattooed & yawning.

We strode the museum together, surveying the seven levels, canvassing the chatty patrons, and never passing a cashier.

Where are we going, Andy Warhol? The doors close in an hour. Which way does your wig point tonight?

Shall we taxi? Or catamaran around the three rivers, ebony and languid? Shall we count the golden bridges until we both fall silent and lonely?

Shall we plainchant of the Pittsburgh of auld lang syne past the dark mills the dark offices the dark condominiums, home to our simple tombs?

Ah, Rusyn brother, pallid pal, weird old impudence-teacher, which Pittsburgh did you see when Charon quit poling his ferry and you debarked on the smoking bank and stood watching his boat slowly vanish over the black waters of the Allegheny?

Andy Warhol for the Widow of Andy Warhol

one cardboard box, sealed, of personal effects
form letter (8 1/2 x 11), aniline purple pigment, ditto machine

The New York Hospital
525 East 68th Street
New York, N.Y. 10021
February 27, 1987

Dear Mrs. Warhol:
We deeply regret the passing
of Andy Warhol. I am writing
in reference to his personal

belongings. As I am sure
you are aware, we are unable
to care for personal property
for a prolonged period of time.

It would be most helpful to us
if you would contact me by either
telephone or mail at your earliest
convenience concerning your wishes

regarding disposition of these
effects. We appreciate your
attention to these matters at what
we know is a difficult time for you.

Sincerely, Dennis Rand, Manager,
Information Department.

Andy Warhol for Undergraduates

after Mike

Before blogger puked & lost it (dorm's DSL crashed!!!),
I saved my post in MSWord, yet somehow got screwed.
PC rebooted, but where's my precious post? Poof-poof!
Gone. My blog was done, damn it, bitching on Jameson's

"The Cultural Logic of Late Capitalism." I'm a neophyte
to Postmodernism and prayed for insight, but is this essay
impenetrable or what? 8 pages in, my eyes glazed over
and I got pissed, cause the guy writes for academicians—

not a good text, Ms. Prof, for Postmodernism 101! That said,
I'll examine 2 famous paintings we discussed in class:
Warhol's *Diamond Dust Shoes* and Vincent Van Gogh's
A Pair of Boots. Van G. paints a pair of peasant boots

in bright colors with mad attention to detail, light, & shadow.
His intention is sympathy & affection for working classes.
Warhol's print, in contrast, is flat, monochromatic: pairs
of various & sundry elongated pointy-pointy pretty shoes.

While Van G. paints details & details galore, Warhol obscures
most pointy-pointy detail intentionally with his lackluster
dimensionality & diversity of palette. In class, I submitted
the theory Van G. selects a symbol of the peasant and elevates

it to nobility, while Warhol is the contrarian. He critiques
the high & bourgeois classes, whose "Diamond Shoes"
he renders to flat, affectless "dust" with his posterizing effect.
But as Warhol was a famously obsessed celebraholic

of the rich & the beautiful, who knows what he's saying?
Guy's got a foot fetish or two? It's easy, but a mistake
to dismiss Warhol as simplistic & meaningless. Unlike
Modernism, which I understand is pretty obvious in message

& intention, Postmodernism is more-than-a-little difficult
& requires inspired work to dig at meaning, it being a reaction
& criticism of Modernism. Warhol is intentionally all surface
& blank & affectless. Viewers must question what Warhol is

trying to say. Is he merely showcasing iconic Americana
cause the artist wants to venerate & celebrate pointy-pointy
shoes? Or is a cynical critique of ads & celebrity lurking
in Warhol's work? I'm not going to pretend to understand

much about Warhol and his artistic intentions, because I don't.
To use a cliché, Andy Warhol is like an onion: I can accept him
& his art at face value & enjoy them at that level, but dig deep
and Warhol morphs for me: more complicated, interesting, & dark

he becomes both as a person & an artist. I chatted with my pal,
and artist who graduated from UW, about our class last week.
I wish he could have been here to offer his insight. Maybe he'll pity
us and write a post here about Warhol and spare us all a headache.

Goodnight. Late for even me.
Posted by Mike at 02:20.

Source: http://metajizz.blogspot.com/2006/11/postmodernism-your-my-big-crybaby-sic.html

Andy Warhol for the *Village Voice* Classifieds, 1966

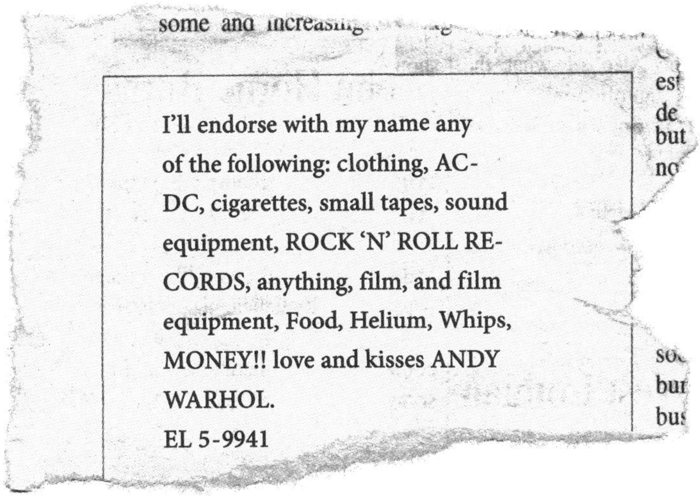

I'll endorse with my name any of the following: clothing, AC-DC, cigarettes, small tapes, sound equipment, ROCK 'N' ROLL RECORDS, anything, film, and film equipment, Food, Helium, Whips, MONEY!! love and kisses ANDY WARHOL.
EL 5-9941

Andy Warhol for *Familiar Quotations*

Andy Warhol said, *Always leave them wanting less.*
Being born, Warhol said, *is like being kidnapped.*
Everyone will be famous, Andy said, *for 15 minutes.*
I thought everyone was just kidding, said Andy.

Being born, Andy Warhol said, *is like being kidnapped.*
Think rich, said Warhol, *look poor.*
I thought everyone was just kidding, said Andy.
Dying, Andy said, *is the most embarrassing thing.*

Think rich, said Andy Warhol, *look poor.*
I am a deeply superficial man, said Warhol.
Dying, Andy said, *is the most embarrassing thing.*
Andy said, *I'd like my tombstone to be blank.*

I am a deeply superficial man, said Andy Warhol.
Fashions fade, Warhol said, *but style is eternal.*
Andy said, *I'd like my tombstone to be blank.*
Isn't life, said Andy, *a series of images that repeat?*

Fashions fade, Andy Warhol said, *but style is eternal.*
Everyone will be famous, Warhol said, *for 15 minutes.*
Isn't life, said Andy, *a series of images that repeat?*
Andy said, *Always leave them wanting less.*

Isn't life, said Andy, *a series of images that repeat?*
Isn't life, said Andy, *a series of images that repeat?*

Always leave them wanting less, Andy said.

Warhol, Andy for Indexers

ambition of, 12–16; autopsy of, 595; as bachelor, 127; "book" vs. "market" value of, 229–30; biographical confusion, 46; British opinion on, 451; capitalization of, 96–100; Carpatho-Rusyn background of, 3–11; and Catholicism, 46–47; "childish mind," 112; Christmas shopping sprees, 310; Coca Cola, 173; cock drawings, 169; as con man, 254; as concert producer, 6; decision not to decide, 7; as diarist (see *Andy Warhol Diaries, The*); dirty-movie admonishment of, 196; dislike of the flesh and touching, 258; dogs (Archie and Amos), 290; drugs, 131, 146, 168, 204; dyslexia, 111, 211; eccentric eating jags, 283; estate valuation of, 352; fame sought, 102; fan clubs of, 168; fear of hospitals, 222; fear of sleep at night, 101, 104; first *success de scandale*, 47; functional boredom, 246; hard-edge style, rejection of, 218; homosexuality of, 6–7, 13, 41–46; house staff of, 155; inability to drive, 135; incapable of saying no, 207; income of, 104; IRS audits, 273; interview style, 2–3; mythic attribution of, 4; name change of, 48; narcissism, 54–55; New Age spirituality, 125–26; nose job, 180; postage stamp issued for, 593; press coverage of, 486-87; psychiatry, 115–16; revolutionary impact of, 3–5; soup kitchen volunteer, 341; strategic use of enigma, 130; tombstone of, 352; voyeur, 11.

from *Definitions*
(1990)

The Story of Glass

From the holes of the earth, from
truck, from silo, from cullet,
from scale, batch, tank, heat-wind; from

heat, from ribbon, from flow, roll
roll, from lehr, they feed the line.

They cross-cut, snap, they flour lites,
plates, plates, plates on belts, coveys,
glass, glass you grab, you pull, you

lift, you pack, you kick, you count,
and you turn, they feed the line.

You reach, you grab, you pack, you
tap, into skid, into crane,
into pack, uncut and cut-

down, they stock, they bay, they stack
skid, skid on skid, box, and they

feed the line. They multi-cut,
they Race 1, they feed you glass
and it comes, it waits, you pack,

it moves, stops, and you pack, it
comes, it comes, it comes without

pause, it comes without thought, it
comes without Jesus or Marx,
it comes, it comes, you pack, they

feed the line. You band, you crimp,
you ship to Kuwait, Detroit,

to Crestline, Ohio, they
profit, it comes, they feed the
line. You eat, you sleep, you bail

glass from your dreams, you drown, you
faint, you rest, you rage, you love,

they feed, they feed
the line, glass, industry you,
from earth.

One of Many Bars in Ford City, Pennsylvania

Some call this home
because they go to Pittsburgh and leave Pittsburgh

saying Pittsburgh makes them nervous.
It is the speed of the line today

for Kijowski, Valasek, and Dietz
gulping beer like air.

For the melancholic three stools down
it is leaky gutters, and the grim

acceptance of a fast line next shift.
It is no guarantee of a line next year.

It's home because Wolsonovich had a heart attack
a week ago Tuesday, and the man working down

from you now you've hated since high school.
For God's sake, let's sit on these stools

and tell sad stories
of the deaths of common men.

My Father

My father was four years in the war,
and afterward, according to my mother,
had nothing to say. She says he trembled
in his sleep the next four years.
My father was twice the father of sons
miscarried, and afterward said nothing.
My mother keeps this silence also.
Four times my father was on strike,
and according to my mother; had nothing
to say. She says the company didn't understand,
nor can her son, the meaning
of an extra fifteen cents an hour in 1956
to a man tending a glass furnace in August.

I have always remembered him a tired man.
I have respected him like a guest
and expected nothing.
It is April now.
My life lies before me,
enticing as the woman at my side.
Now, in April, I want him to speak.
I want to stand against the worn body
of his pain. I want to try it on
like a coat that does not fit.

Family Portrait, 1933

In the center my grandfather sits
a patriarch, a boy on his knee
and children surrounding. His face says
this is my contribution, but the lips want
reassurance. My grandmother is a trunk
of a woman three children wide,
her face stern and unfathomable.

While they are stiff and attentive,
I want to speak: Father, little Father,
we are both twenty now. Hear me.
You will lease your body to machines
like the man did
on whose shoulder you rest your hand.
After forty years you'll whisper,
"I'm just an old man smoking cigarettes
in the cellar, fixing radios."
Uncles, aunts, I can't keep track of you.
Live.
Grandfather, Grandmother, don't worry.
I'll be born in twenty-two years
and grow strong and bury you.
Uncle Mike, old mole,
you will bury yourself
in the coalfields of Pennsylvania.
Please resume now.
Come unfrozen, quickly;
do what you must do.

Landscape with Unemployed, 1934

What we feel
has to do with the air
so sweet
it is sickening.

Has to do with the air
so clear
it is sickening.
We march arm in arm

so clear
in the street of lilies.
We march arm in arm
wearing sober hats

in the street of lilies,
singing, "No jobs! No jobs!"
wearing sober hats,
the radical priests

singing, "No jobs! No jobs!"
casting shadows,
the radical priests
who celebrate us, and sing us,

casting shadows
the color of burnt earth,
who celebrate us, and sing us,
as we lean and loaf,

the color of burnt earth.
We loaf and invite our souls.
We lean and loaf
on the summer grass,

loaf and invite our souls—
born here
on the summer grass—
hoping they'll never cease.

Born here,
we watch flames opening,
hoping they'll never cease
and we hurry along the street.

We watch flames opening
all the windows
and we hurry along the street,
our shadows sticking.

All the windows
of where we worked, burning,
our shadows sticking
to the burnt earth

of where we worked, burning.
Such shadows, Van Gogh said,
must be daubed on with a knife.
The burnt earth.

Our shadows sticking.
What we feel,
no jobs, no jobs,
what we feel.

The Annual PPG Pensioners' Picnic

When I awoke it was almost dark, the sun
half-sunk, silent and purple. I remember the pungent
dampness, the rot of needles, the scent of sausage
lifting me as I trudged along the path
a little woozy, a little twisted with sleep.
Look—Father Korba was dealing now and telling jokes
he had learned on retreat, but none of them in English.
My grandfather clicked his teeth.
"Come on, come on now!" he muttered,
his sandwich in one hand, his cards in the other.
For just a minute I felt pure. For maybe the first time
I felt lucid and sentimental about his straw hat,
about his white socks, about his pony bottles of beer,
his Hunky music wafting over from the grove.
I babbled at him and waved my arms and kissed him
on both cheeks. We set off for the parking lot
to consider the winter of 1913 and the fat years
after the second war. We danced a little
in the cinders, in the glow from the rim of the sky.
We watched the valley stretch
below us and the river wind away for miles and the bats
shriek and dip below the bridge.
We crossed ourselves, moaning, "God preserve us!"
under the moon rising small and thin,
as the mill fumed, as the town glimmered, as the star ignited
above it, burning like a carefully carried candle.

After the Deindustrialization of America, My Father Enters Television Repair

My hands hold, my father's solder the wires—
picture rolls once, then steadies . . . an English castle!
A voice-over drones about Edward I,
who, to subdue the Welsh, built castles.
Some sixty years, dozens of engineers, the masses
conscripted from the villages.

My father moves on to a Zenith
with a bad tuner. TVs interest him, not the English
with their damp, historical programming.

* * *

Here there were Indians, mound builders.
Here, an English fort, a few farmers.
And here the industrialist settled his ass,
John Ford on the river dredging sand
for making glass. Plate glass.
(Why should America buy from Europe?)
Some half dozen years, German engineers, and hundreds of Slavic peasants.

Grandfather sat on his samovar
warming himself and making excuses,
but finally, he set off.
Got a room, became a shoveler.
Got a wife, a company house.
Ford City: a valley filling with properties.

No one got along—
Not Labor and Capital, not Germans and Slavs,
not husbands and wives, for that matter.

* * *

Edward's castles were ruins
by the fifteenth century. Not from Welsh armies,
but the rise of the middle class.
The towns around a castle thrived:
tailors, smithies, cobblers, coopers.
Drawing in the Welsh peasants.
And what with intermarriage and the rise of capitalism . . .
a castle grew obsolescent.

I turn off the set. My father hunts
cigarettes at the Kwik-Mart on the corner.
Overhead, my mother's footsteps,
the tonk of bottles,
the scraping of plates.

* * *

During Eisenhower's reign
my grandfather retired and mowed his lawn
until I took over. He primed the filter,
set the choke, then we took turns pulling
till the sputtering engine caught.
("Somanabitch," he spit)
And watched me as I mowed
back and forth for two dollars.

Once in the garage he showed me a scythe.
He mowed hay in the old country, and the women
would follow, raking it in windrows.

* * *

The factories today are mostly closed down,
or full of robots or far off in Asia.
Ford City lives through the mail:
compensation, a thin pension,
and, of course, Social Security.

I always drive along the factory, windows rolled down;
I want my kids in the back seat to see.
Seven or eight, probably pensioners, congregate
on the corner, each man dressed quite alike:
Sears jacket, cigarette, salt-and-pepper hair.

"Honk the horn," my oldest begs.
He waves and waves zealously
until a man turns—a man
with my face, but full of sweetness now,
silence and clarity.

The Social Impact of Corporate Disinvestment

Pittsburgh, Toledo, Chicago, Detroit.
Uncle Paul changed mills like shoes,
Aunt Sophie dragging behind, dragging
their six weepy daughters.
He ended finally in Kansas, in General Motors,
where his bad heart caught up to him.

My cousins called the priest,
the undertaker, and the doctor,
who gave Sophie a little something.
It was November then.
The stars could barely shine
through the Presbyterian heavens.
Somehow desire, like a cyclone,
swept over the prairie, over her flat life,
confused her.
                    She walked out
naked into a field beyond the garage.
Threw herself flat.
Embraced the earth without a tear.

The sun had long since risen
by the time she returned home.
"Mother!" they all wailed, and promptly
put her to bed, pale and waxen.
The priest was summoned.

When he had finished the prayer
of the dying over her, she sat up,
quite cheerful, and from her pillow
withdrew a ten. His stipend.

They all looked at each other and looked
at each other—and drifted to the kitchen
for the poppy seed and nut rolls and coffee.

Toward the Heaven of Full Employment

Out of love for the dead Kennedys,
    out of fear of her laid-off spouse,
Aunt Sophie lit candles and prayed an extra rosary
    so God would make the payment on the house.

Even then factories like carriers at sea
    steamed off toward the Far East.
Even then the men, paging magazines,
    smoked more, grew bored and obese.

Mock on, mock on, Mr. Marx and Mr. Engels,
    this America of the idle and decadent.
Haul us up, slow God, speed us like angels
    toward the heaven of full employment.

Now

Now the silence. Now the peace.
Now the empty hands uplifted. And my father, now
the pensioner, recites a psalm before
the icon, addresses praise to the cloudy
forehead of God.
                                        Now the morning, all crammed with
heaven, and the mystery of cigarettes and coffee.
Behind the cup and smoke, behind the radio's low mutter
he empties his head, turning more inward hourly.
I want said what needs said: his story wide and long now,
a public account, out of the furnace of the private life.
I want to trust it, to own it, to sit between boredom
and wonder watching it rise beneath the dome of stars, over
the tender years, over the wars, over the mill's crooked
gloom, the long arcs rising, rising toward the triumphant,
toward the end of historical time. I want his silence
broken now and what is mine.

No, he says, *I have no story.*
The story tells me. Even now.

Tolstoy in Heaven

The full shoulders and bosoms
of women in low-necked gowns
are not a problem here.

His other lust? God?
Like two bears in one lair,
Lev Nikolayevich and He.
Look at them playing cards.
Tolstoy, in dead earnest,
holds his cards like a live bird.

Hands like these, forever . . .

Agnes McGurrin

May your death cause no one pleasure.
—Irish proverb

She can't sleep.
After ten years in a shirt factory
and a marriage of forty years,
after kids, strikes, boredom—
        more kids.
After grandkids, after stroke,
after St. Jude's Home for Diocesan Infirmed,
she can't sleep.
Only this: an image

of late August, a maple losing its leaves.
Her children look consumptive. Thin as twigs.
Here's a table, a bee, a bushel of pears.
They peel easily, smell sweet.
She reaches for a jar and her breasts fall
plump and fragrant into the bushel.
The bee circles her head, Agnes hurries
to finish canning. Her breasts fall again:
pears, more pears . . .
She's flustered, the bee still circling,
then it lights on her wrist. Winter blooms
white as an orchid; a wind stings her awake.

Her husband drops her roughly into the wheelchair
these mornings, and soon he's gone to play cards.
A morning game, pensioners only.
She remembers the club young. Battle of bands.
There was swing, then a slow number.

Lots of smoke and hugging. They'd come early
to see the sand sprinkled on the dance floor.
A handful of sugar to make it smooth.

Agnes starts a letter to her daughter.
She wants to write about *purpose,* but
two cardinals sing from tomato stakes. She's gone
rolling down the wide aisle of her garden.
The birds fly. She begins the ritual
watering, plunging her cupped hand again and again
into the pail, relaxing her fingers over the beans.

Agnes thinks to herself.
A neighbor's phone rings. A bus rumbles past.
She can hardly hear herself,
just a TV preacher voice
through an open window, singing.

The Jeweler

He always repaired a cross and chain free.

Once he outfitted our basketball team
with Holy Infant of Prague medals; he insisted
they were the difference in '37 against Frackville.
He was floating in for a lay-up
when number 22, a Methodist, grabbed his chain,
choking him silly. He got so angry
he changed the score by himself.

Someone told me he worked in the mill one day.
Just walked out.
Left for watch repair school in Scranton.

On his gravestone is carved a small clock
and on each side a flowering vine.
At least that's how his brother, a sandblaster,
has worked it out. Before the last trumpet
that clock should ring and ring and ring.

At a Jewish Cemetery in Pittsburgh

Someone is looking for us.
I sensed it earlier at the creek
while floating on my back, and again
on Route 8 near Brookline.
So we've detoured to this hillside
eroding and crazy with markers.
We're looking for row *mm* or *nn*
or something like that.
I lug the baby; my wife runs ahead.
This neighborhood knows her—
she passes so easily between stones.
She finds the grave, her father
dead ten years now. In the time it takes
to say kaddish the sun's dropped.
I set down my son
and he crawls in the dimness,
pulling himself up on the headstone.
How delicately he fingers the marble.
Quickly he rounds its corner. Vanishes.
I'm thinking: *grass, stone, quiet*—
then babbling from another world.

Pleasure

Three weeks after Christmas,
the toy piano with its joyous popping frogs
sat silent for three days, and my boy
lay beside it sucking his thumb,
having found there, staring in,
the boredom in all pleasure, and
the sadness of a beautiful thing.

About My Son and Hands

This month, our son's fourth, he is studying hands
with much reverence and drooling. The books insist
on *more dangling toys, a spoon to play with,*
but the little man prefers a father's knuckle
or his mother's sweet thumb, and especially the joining
of his own two hands. The clumsy fingers of one explore
those of the other; the grasp, the squeezing
tell him they are dear friends for life.
From his walker his supple spine *dahvens,*
then he raises his hands like a rabbi,
milking the long ceremonious moment, then they drop
to his toothless smile and consonant laugh.
When he rests them on his yellow tray,
it is with authority. The hands emissaries now,
ready to accept the small objects we offer.

Poem for Hamid

1.

Dawn: the sky whitens.
All night the blue factories clanked & whirred,
thickening the air.
Yet this is a morning,
and this is a grapefruit, this sugar.
This is a key, a car; this is torque
and we move.

This is North America. Have a nice day.
This is not hell, it's a supermarket.
See the lettuce: bib, leaf, iceberg, romaine.
This is not death, it's fried chicken.
Taste it. It has taste.

2.

Letter from Abroad, May 1981
The left disappears. Many are underground and the prisons are full. Some mornings the gunshots wake us. Fadwa will rush out of bed, dress, chatter about getting work, but I linger. I am writing leaflets, translating, smoking too much. No word yet from Ali. Mother worries and busies herself cooking.

3.

Remember the time we were taken to jail?
Posting leaflets illegally.
Getting out by morning—my only concern—

while you were lost in study:
how two kids in for robbery paced,
how they couldn't fill out the forms.

Drunk or dumb? What did it matter?
I think of the green walls peeling,
the one toilet, the chill that floated in
from the hall.
What makes you believe
everyone lives to some purpose?

4.

That is my son
pulling himself up on the chair leg.
That is his word, *bup,* sailing
in this comfortable room.
What here is not to like?
What?

5.

Letter from Ali, July 1981
I am living in a northern province. No running water, no electricity, nothing like the undergraduate life I loved in Denver. The new regime has no influence here. I am hidden by a good family; from my window I watch them going about each day. The women must knock away shit with a stick before drawing water. Crops are poor. Oil does us little good without rainfall. Some days I wonder how we'll change what the centuries have not touched.

6.

Hamid, that your grief were my life
or my life your grief, is academic.
The lawn fertilizer I do not buy
may never reach your country.
We do what we can. No regrets.
This is still a life, not grief.
Still life.

After the Movement

Reading,
weary again.
I think of Marx's eyes:
hard, indefatigable pepper-
corns.

Outside, sprinklers
whir and spin, persistent
as the March of Dimes
volunteer. *I give, I give.*
These books are sunlight

trapped in clear jars—limp light.
A person could live fishing
or berrying. Some life.
No, I want to be that squirrel
bounding across the high voltage wire

while kids on skates, kids in cars,
rage below.
Moonlight: lead me over.

Extreme Unction

"There is no God," Father Korba said,
"like the silence of a man's own house."
Old Shevchenko, mostly bones, lay there dead.
"God is here," Korba said.
The widow set a table: candles, salt, and bread.

Half the night we sat with her
till I began to drowse:
my mind a wide cloud, passing from the head
through the rooms of the silent house.

Old Shevchenko

I recall him, plainly, in his black wool suit
and his yellow shirt buttoned at the collar.

After evening bells, he'd stroll
until dark, and at corners
he'd quote from the Gospel; a mumble
on the breeze, an angel in black,
drawing laughs from passersby.

I saw him once encircled by *Los Barbados*,
seven bearded men on motorcycles. He glared
at their skull-and-bone insignias.
Pocketing his bifocals, he unbuttoned his shirt
and doffed his black fedora. From his neck
he lifted a block of painted wood—
the icon of the Black Madonna.
It dangled
from a boot lace, then he shook it at them
and passed from their midst unharmed.

This was in the sixties, when I was a boy
and given to searching for signs. I looked
to the sky, to crumbling gray clouds,
where the blue appeared like a beautiful eye.

I sat and looked around me
and listened. The leaves overhead
scarcely rustled; by their delicate noise
I have trusted my life.

An American Peace

1.

In my dream I'm seven and dependable,
shopping for Mother, who must hang clothes.
I buy lamb at Shevchenko's, the good butcher
who believes in me, trusts me with change,
a pack of Luckies, and I ride off,
groceries steady, over the paved, black alley.

It is the bald head that stops me.
And bushy brows—of my principal
fumbling in his fob pocket . . .
the siren wails, the drill begins:
I'm running from school past the dry cleaner's,
past the plumber's, past the travel agency,
leaping hedges and dodging bombs
to reach the shelter, St. Mary's
Ukrainian Catholic Church.
                                        Here Grandmother,
rag-fisted, dusts the icons of mystics
and martyrs. St. Stephen darts out;
smoke issues from his lips: "Depart!
Catechumen, depart!" I run
to the dark basement. The glowing cigar
is Father Korba. He hums a hymn,
focuses the filmstrip *Paradise Lost:*
where the sun, red and angry, scowls down
over the trees, and animals in bushes glower;
where an angel drives us with his fiery sword
to the east where all things fade.
In the last frame Adam hunches

over a crude wooden plow; his massive oxen lumber.
God follows in the furrows,
but Adam believes it's the wind. Only wind.
Eve—her hair blown back—stares
from the clearing's edge, baby at breast.

2.

When I think of my mother,
she is always hanging clothes.
My father is on the couch,
sleeping off the factory
and saying *No.* He opens one eye
to say *No.*

* * *

On TV, Torako Nakamachi:
who remembers burned work clothes,
glass fragments, a burning pine tree.
Naked girls crying, "Stupid America!"
She remembers a woman walking as her skin trailed,
and another crouched at the river, her breasts torn.

* * *

I stepped onto a streetcar of the Hakushi line. I heard the bell, felt the car jerk, then the sky flashed white. I jumped to the track and braced myself. The heat, a whooshing sound swept over me. When I stood I was in a crowd, everyone reeling, naked, and colliding.

I pulled my air raid dress from my bag, tugged it on, tied my hair back with a kerchief. Black rain fell. A boy walked past, his head bloated like a boiled octopus.

"My husband," I thought. But I felt no loneliness. I walked. I remember a horse running and in flames. I remember two boys in the street cooling their burnt mother with paper fans. A piece of wood stuck out of the mother's eye, and one son placed a cucumber in her hand. I walked past the middle school, shouts of "To the river!" and "God help me!" and "Water! Water!" I remember a corpse on its back, hand turned upright, fingers burning with blue flames. I walked on and heard a small voice pleading. Four or five quickly gathered, but we could not push the concrete from the old man's chest. I turned away whispering, "Forgive me, little Father."

* * *

In the Buddhist temple dormitory
a woman moaned from her cot, her jaw gone.
When she moved her mouth, it resembled
a cracked watermelon.
Many died.

Torako, on her cot, watched the days pass;
watched hair turn brown-red and fall;
watched the gums and nails bleed;
watched the burns on backs
swell into sacks of water.
Like so many peddlers, she thought.
Sacks of water on their backs.

3.

On his back my father carried a pack
of forty pounds, and jungled in tropical forests,
hopping islands north toward Japan.

The generals wanted strips—concrete
in the bush for landing planes.

When working once, about midday,
the sky filled with men.
        "Maybe three dozen
Japs floated down, almost pretty. We ran
for guns, tried to kill them
before they hit. We radioed for reinforcements,
but they'd be days in coming.
All I wanted? To walk *this* town again,
where no one in a hundred years would shoot me."

Once I leaned against a garage door
and longed for blood to my name.
Soroka's father had it, Monchak's too.
A dozen Japs dropped by them alone.
I held their war souvenirs:
shiny medals, a dagger, even a gold tooth!
"Got 'em off dead Japs," Soroka puffed.
"I got more at the house."

That night I followed my father
into the cellar and watched him repair a TV.
I wanted to know if he'd killed a man.
Ever killed a man.
        He looked up,
the smoke of his cigarette between us.
"I don't know," he said.
"You just shoot, you never know."

4.

1967: I wake and walk
downstairs, lie on the couch,
my head in my mother's lap.
She lets me sleep a little longer,
strokes my hair and murmurs her prayers.
I sleep—how I sleep—buoyant
in her rhythm and the radio's beat.

I eat, then walk to Mass,
to the vestry where Korba greets me,
"Slava Isusu Christu!"
"Glory forever!" I reply. I help him
to vest: alb, stole, cincture, chasuble.
We stand ready, both in black,
to offer the unbloody sacrifice.

The censer smokes, the bells peal,
and Korba, in a sweet cloud, sings Slavonic:
Blahoslovenno carstvo, Otca i Syna . . .
"Blessed be the kingdom, blessed be . . ."
We chant for good weather, for abundance
of the fruits of the earth,
for an angel of peace, a faithful guide,
a guardian of our souls and bodies.
We chant for goodness to descend—
that we may spend our days in peace,
gaining a painless, blameless,
simple end, and a good account
before the judgment seat.

5.

Polish Falcon Park, 1968,
and Hubert Horatio Humphrey.
Rev. Korba, ethnic priest, posed for *Newsweek*:
hugging Humphrey, stumping for Humphrey,
kissing him upon each cheek,
under bunting, under banners unfurling
"Good Day! *Dobri Den!*"
They shook hands, talked Vietnam
and new jobs for our valley.

That whole year I followed him
in *Newsweek*: Humphrey in color, the war in color,
maps, graphs, opinion polls.

Then November and Nixon won . . .
and my brother Bob was drafted.
We are not soldiers, I thought.
We are bright. Bright students.
They expected a doctor, a lawyer, a priest.
As Father Korba had once told Mother:
"A life, your boys deserve a life
of books and difficult reading."

Thanksgiving. And Bob
with his decision not to go.

6.

A mouthful to say, but the thought simple:
Conscientious objection.
                                        Not bombs.

Self-determination for the people
of Vietnam. And peace.

“You still with me?” asked Bob.

Something about his eyes, something
about his hands gesturing—
like Korba, I thought.
Speaking with authority. Self-assured.
The luminous vision taking over . . .

I loved my brother for his long hair
and monkish sandals, but hated him
for the scandal that ensued:
“Your brother’s yellow. And Red.
And behaving like a Red Jew.”

He left me without facts
or adequate arguments,
just a dim vision of the global village
where I was welcome everywhere.
In Hanoi, for example, they would love me
for my sneakers, love me for my jeans.
Love unconditional:
because I was peaceful as they were peaceful,
one with them, the dispossessed
rising and innumerable,
bent on justice, bent on peace,
with whom I’d sit under vine and fig tree
and make joyful noises;
with whom I’d dance in a great circle,
all of us reconciled—

Korba and Mao, Humphrey and Ho—
everyone a bit teary for what's passed
and done with.
We would start singing, our voices
uneven at first, not sounding from the chest,
but growing, little by little,
each of us feeling the wave of sweetness
and shivery anticipation
for the song as it swells, soon to overflow . . .

But what about the Bomb?

"The Japs wouldn't quit," my mother recalled,
"and we were ready to invade.
Would have been your dad
on some beach, probably dead."

She worked the evening shift
making windshields for the bombers.
Sirens, she remembers, above the din
of belts and gears, then bells,
beautiful bells pealing.

And she was sent home,
the machines still running . . .

7.

Father Korba is teaching:
"So why is there suffering?"
His tobacco-stained fingers
running through his silver hair.

We are stumped.
"By Adam's fall . . .
we sinned all," hints Father.

We're speechless.

Then Beck—
who sits near a window to spit—
snaps, "What's that mean?"

So Korba preaches on the Pelagians.
Augustine thought he'd finished them off,
but no, they're back,
with that doctrine of Original Righteousness,
the infant a cute, blank tablet.
"The world is like an aquarium,"
Father says, "like a *poisoned* aquarium.
Soon as you're born, you suck it in."

He has preached this before
at baptisms and at funerals,
so I know what line is next:
"There's a worm in the human heart."
The whole class giggles, squirms.
And Korba stops, his chest heaving.

8.

When Korba prayed, it was for the Iron Curtain
to crumble, for Communism to wither
like the fig tree cursed by Christ.

He prayed for the bodies of our people
in the East, who must queue up for meat,
our separated brethren living under

Lenin, under his pure materialism
and the neo-czars.
Korba, clear and rigid,

denounced our enemies each Sunday:
atheists, Protestants,
sons of Freud, Rousseau, and Marx

who ran television and the dirty movies,
taught at universities
to lead young Catholics astray.

Disciples of human nature
think they can straighten the world,
but we know better, he said.

The self is flawed.
Curiously flawed.
We need God to lift us.

Or maybe this war will do.
We need God, he said, need God
to fill these pews.

9.

In *Esquire, The New Yorker,*
even in the Sunday supplement,
I read how America may end in fire
and how the president prepares for it.
While we lie down or stand up,
while we swim or jog
or watch movies on the cable,
the president thinks, consults,
plans for any and every contingency.
He must be smart, be tough,
be thinking in fists of thought,
because a specter is haunting the world.

The president is thinking
rationing will go smoothly:
meat, milk, fuel, grains.
Underground, toughing it out.

At 30,000 feet, the president
circles and circles and circles.
He thinks: *Federal Reserve.*
He thinks: *Plan A or Plan B.*
He thinks: *Post-attack inflation.*

The president thinks and trucks emerge
from hollowed-out mountains.
If roads are bad, he thinks: *four-wheel drive.*

10.

In this third year of Reagan, my twenty-seventh year,
I dreamed we walked the warehouses
of the lower North Side, down to the Ohio

where we stripped. In a purple mist,
through shimmery waters, we stroked out,
borne up by small waves,

and at midstream I faced Pittsburgh,
West End bridge at my back, to one side
Stephanie, to the other my first son,

only our heads above water, bobbing
and bobbing, when in front of us he surfaced,
Jacob, our youngest, and it seemed

that from his head, his large infant head,
the skyline loomed, the sun upsprung behind
like a brilliant furnace;

tower and office and condominium
blazed red, radiant, forming a crown
of sorts, a wild wig of city,

so that we laughed.
Then the sky flashed white
as if the sun had dropped closer:
one second, two seconds, three seconds,
blast: deafness, ringing, Jacob's screaming:

I reached, saw my hands, saw the bones of my hands
and saw Jacob dig at his eyes, screaming . . .
which I couldn't stop or relieve, but I grabbed him,
thinking water, dunked him
and held him hard.
                                        I turned to the cloud
mushrooming, the light in pinks and blues,
all the while wrestling Jacob, whom I could no longer hear.
A whooshing sound started, heat-wind in a wave,
and I was driven under, accelerated through black waters,
giddy with fear until I loosened my grip,
relaxed my shoulders, my neck,
and my whole body lightened, rarefied,
the blackness through me and with me and in me,
when my mind like a dim flashlight
began to sweep in search of something—
something recognizable—
but there was nothing, only
water and the mind aware of itself.

11.

All shall be well
and all shall be well
and all manner of thing shall be well.
No matter what.
                                    Said Lady Julian of Norwich,
the English mystic, as quoted by a Japanese nun
I saw on television.

This nun smiles

during the whole documentary;
one suspects her face is paralyzed.
But the interviewer doesn't relent,
makes her call up from hell
what she witnessed that day
in Hiroshima, where her convent crumbled
and where she walked away intact—
as if guided by some steady angel.
She is happy now in Los Angeles
in her new convent.
As for the others,
she does not worry, but trusts
to the presence of grace.
All shall be well.

12.

I will probably go up
to Warren, Pennsylvania.
Aunt Olga has a cabin there
sheltered by the mountains,
with its own clear spring,
a trout stream nearby,
plenty of berries and wild edibles
my wife knows so much about.

Urged to leave our city, we pack
the kids in—speed past the zoo,
past the mall, past the industrial park,
finally free of the north suburbs.
We stop in Ford City:

my mother banging on the door
of her neighbor, a woman from Slovakia
who has locked herself in.

We crowd into the Toyota,
Father shouting about an article
on electromagnetic pulse. EMP.
The Russians may try one nuke
over Nebraska, far up in space,
the whole country bathed
with it, not harming a soul,
just circuits.
Not a dial tone left
even for the president.

Just off a back road
near Warren, Pennsylvania,
we sit in our cabin,
stare at the worn linoleum
and the furniture from the fifties.
Waiting for something to happen . . .
guessing if the Burger King is open in town,
and whether to risk it and the ethics
of the new social disorder.
Waiting for chaos. And pestilence.
Maybe typhoid, cholera, or dreaded Q fever.
Sitting and chatting, preparing our minds.
Growing more compatible with each other
and more companionable with our death.

13.

I am the man at noon
on the sidewalk downtown.
In face paint, in black tux,
I balance on a silver tray
a model Cruise missile.
                                        "Order this?"
I say, shuffling
between the secretaries and CPAs
I am a week in prayer and fasting
with Molly Rush and Daniel Berrigan.
We use false badges
to enter AVCO Systems Division,
bang warhead mounts with tiny hammers,
pour baby bottles of our own blood,
sing, "Rejoice! Rejoice!
Again I say rejoice!"

In my quiet moods I write a book,
Thoughts on the Threat.
But the *Times* critic carries on
about its adolescent logic,
how its author has never heard
even a small mortar explode.
"Such books have become cliché."

What to do then?
I am a North American
from the soft belly of comfort,
from state of the art, from hi-tech;
my poems in part possible

by a generous grant from the state.
And it is good, mostly.

Today we drove like demons
up and down the Miracle Mile
to compare floor patterns, refrigerators,
advanced technology stoves.
I'd like a new kitchen
because I want to eat through the coming winter;
because the economy needs fed;
because the machines need the work;
because it's my way of defending against
all death and non-being.

I will celebrate my new stove
for the light and heat it gives,
a sign that someone loves us,
some stovemaker, if not God,
who has made it for our pleasure
with glass door and chrome finish,
with continuous cleaning oven,
with timer, beeper, and pilotless
ignition, saving energy, my energy.
Saving it for leisure.

I am convinced that one day
they'll have it all figured out.
Those lab coats at Harvard
and in the halls of MIT.
I will peer into the microscope with them,
confirm it with them,

that Death is a cellular defect.
We will tune-up our DNA and RNA
adding years to our lifespan.

I do not need the president
with his manuscript on the rostrum,
with his hints of impatience for the applause to die down.
I do not want his speech about circling up the wagons.
I do not need his war to feel that high moment
of community.

We have our own hope,
structured into our genes.
For ages it has talked to us and kept us
on the narrow ridge of faith,
as we sat by the rivers of Babylon;
as we sat in the Dark Ages;
as we sat in the stone cathedrals;
as we sat in the concrete libraries.
We heard it in the rushing and swirling
of our blood,
in the atoms rotating, the galaxy rotating,
the great rhythm programmed into us
during the morning of the world.
It was a matter of time before we'd walk
through shafts of sunlight and shadow,
to sit down and pass a hand
across our heavy, thick foreheads.
It brought us to consciousness
and to these instruments
where we can see matter's purple flush,

see the glowing within it,
a presence that pulls us in
relieving the terror and the long loneliness.
Four billion years to reach here.
Let's rest awhile. Let us sit.

14.

When I was a boy, we'd climb above town
to sit on the rock shelf
                                        dangling our legs . . .
Spread like a gameboard,
the town would always quiet us—
yards so small . . . as were our mothers
hanging clothes.
It was philosophy to watch
the bread man delivering
and the men out mowing the lawns.
When the mill whistled or the bells rang,
people moved in patterns
making sense from a height,
the back and forth, the in and out,
organizing the world.
                                        Back then a voice
would often sound inside me,
        All shall be well
a voice that was not me,
        and all shall be well
always faint, persistent,
hinting for me to trust . . .
        and all manner of thing shall be well.
        No matter what.

Acknowledgments

Poems from the following previously published books are included in this volume:

> Poems from *Definitions*, copyright © 1990 by Peter Oresick. Reprinted by permission of West End Press.
>
> Poems from *Warhol-O-Rama*, copyright © 2008 by Peter Oresick, reprinted with the permission of The Permissions Company, Inc., on behalf of Carnegie Mellon University Press, www.cmu.edu/universitypress. All rights reserved.

Thanks to the editors of the *Pittsburgh Post-Gazette*, *Great River Review*, and *5 AM* for publishing some of these poems in earlier versions and to Garrison Keillor for featuring work from *Warhol-O-Rama* on National Public Radio's *The Writer's Almanac*. Thanks to the University of Chicago, the Wexner Center for the Arts, the Palmer Museum of Art, and Spencer Museum of Art for installations and exhibitions of poems from *Warhol-O-Rama*. I would like to thank the Heinz Endowments for a fellowship to the Virginia Center for the Creative Arts.

I am indebted to friends who, over the years, have been my first readers and have given me the benefit of their criticism, especially to Ed Ochester, John Crawford, Gerald Costanzo, Gerald Stern, Judith Vollmer, Lawrence Joseph, Gary Metras, Jim Dochniak, Jon Anderson, Lynn Emanuel, Louis Simpson, Patricia Dobler, Paul Zimmer, Samuel Hazo, Jan Beatty, Julia Kasdorf, and Richard St. John.

I have been blessed with a supportive, loving family all of my life—my mother and father, my brothers Robert and Lawrence, and four grandparents created the first nucleus. Marrying Stephanie expanded the circle to include my mother-in-law Edith Flom Schneider and our sons William, Jake, and David. Their pairings brought our daughters Mandi and Deanna and our grandchildren Anna, Adelyn, and William. Aunts, uncles, cousins, in-laws, nieces, nephews, and honorary family members—my life is indeed very full.